The Ten Deadly Realms

By

Venessa Williamson, Deserie Questell

ISBN: 0-75964-274-5

This book is printed on acid free paper.

1stBooks – rev. 10/18/01

Chapter One

In the beginning, many centuries ago, in the highest region of the earth, located near the Crystal Mountains was a heavenly and holy place called Nirvana. This city had golden gates. Engraved on the golden gates was the name, "The City Of Nirvana," which was guarded by two white winged angels who guarded the city.

When you entered the city, it was raining different types of beautiful flowers. Lotuses, pansies, violets, and cherry blossoms. The city of Nirvana itself was laid out like a square. The buildings, monasteries, and streets were pure gold. This city shined so brightly, it was like looking through transparent glass. A river called Everlasting and Eternal Life was a pretty clear color of deep sea blue. On both sides of the river were trees and flowers, each bearing ten different kinds of fruits. There were delicious and plump apples, mangos, pears, grapes, plums, peaches, oranges, tangerines, and nectarines, hanging from each green leaf branch. Precious heirloom gemstones were in a vault.

Nirvana's main temple called the Eternal Throne had ten chambers consisting of warriors, singer, dancers, religious beings of worship, Buddha monks, and the Supreme Being of the universe, who was the highest of all of the people of the city of Nirvana, including the monks, angels and religious beings. Even though this was a place of peace, and religious worship, there was an evil presence that existed. One of the religious beings, called Daylor who was appointed as the high counselor of Nirvana, was getting ideas of his own. He was reading and stealing sacred scrolls, and book documents that nobody was allowed to touch, read, or handle. Sacred knowledge is forbidden, because if it fell into the wrong hands, that person will turn evil instantly, with wicked traits of hatred, vanity, jealousy, hatred in their heart, a warrior, conqueror, and ready to kill at any cause. They will also be in darkness for eternity. Their physical appearance will change to an ugly apparition. And they will not be able to keep their holy name. That is the sacred law of Nirvana. But Daylor, knew all these things, and yet he continued with his evil ways, and curiousity. Using his new found knowledge, he persuaded other members to be on his side to take over the holy city of Nirvana. "My fellow members, now is the time to carry out our plans. We do not need the teachings of the Supreme Being. And we do not have to listen to him because there are a lot of things about power and knowledge that he did not want us to know about. So he has betrayed us." All the followers shouted out loud, "Daylor is telling the truth. We choose him as our new leader who will lead us to take over Nirvana. Let's overthrow the kingdom now, and anybody who rebels against us will be killed!"

The rebels of Daylor were very anxious to overtake the kingdom of Nirvana. For they felt they were right about the Supreme Being and the laws of Nirvana. And they deeply felt that their new leader Daylor would set things straight.

The rebellious attack started at dawn. There were so much killing, and blood shed that morning. Some of the sacred statues, were destroyed. Valuable documents and scrolls were stolen from their protective golden cases. This was an insult and a disgrace to the Buddha gods, to the people of Nirvana, as well as the Supreme Being. No one would have ever thought that this evil would of taken place. "We must fight to the finish! yelled Daylor. If you can kill all the people or take them as slaves, we will win the battle! No one must escape!" Daylor conjured up five three-headed flying serpent snakes with big long fangs, which breathes out fire. The serpent hotly starts to fly all over the place, and began attacking and eating the citizens of Nirvana very viciously. The specially trained warriors of Nirvana had to protect the city and the citizens. The archangels were also summoned by the trained warriors for help, because they knew that Daylor had become very powerful. Malark, who is one of the warriors, yelled out to them, "Continue to fight, while I go and get the fighting archangels!" Immediately, Malark flew as fast as he could to summon the fighting archangels. When he arrived at the golden gate, he told Gabriel the angel what was happening inside the city. At that moment Gabriel blew his horn and all the legions of angels appeared before him. Each angel had white silver robes, and silver wings. Their weapons were flaming swords made of gold and silver. They rushed as fast as they could to help protect the city. It took no time for the powerful archangels to surround the city. The battle even got more uglier as they closed in on Daylor and his tribe of men. Daylor, when he saw them flying towards him and his men, knew that they were defeated. But still he pressed on and continued to fight with all of his might.

"Keep on fighting! Don't let them stop you! We have our flying serpents to help us out!" shouted Daylor. His men continued to fight, not knowing that these archangels were very, very powerful, and that you could not defeat them.

Daylor did not tell them this. He also deceived them by not telling them that he betrayed the Buddha gods, as the well as the people of Nirvana, that all their sacred scrolls were stolen and read by him.

The fight was more bloody than ever. All of Daylor's men, including the deadly serpents charged with all their might at Gabriel and his archangels. They were willing to die for their leader. Soon they would have a new ruler sitting upon the throne at Nirvana. There were a lot of slashing and thrashing of their swords. Even the green and very evil monstrous serpents tore at the angels flesh with their sharp fangs and wrapped their long tails around them to squeeze them to death, but the plan failed. Gabriel, and his legion of archangels slashed and thrashed back at Daylor and his men with their flaming gold and silver swords. These swords were extremely powerful. Too powerful. Heads, arms, legs, and different parts of the body were amputated in a matter of seconds from the sharp and pointed blade of the flaming swords. It was very obvious. The archangels and Gabriel had supernatural powers and strength. They even cut off the tails of the serpents with one blow. "You might as well give up! shouted Gabriel to Daylor and his men. The kingdom of Nirvana will never be ruled by Daylor! You are stupid to believe this! Surrender now, and we will forgive you for your sins, including Daylor." "No! No! shouted Daylor's men to the archangels. We do not accept your offer! You, and the Supreme Being of Nirvana are the ones who have deceived us!" It was no use. The fighting continued on. Daylor was not giving up. He had too much to lose. With one last effort, Daylor raised his arms over his head and he concentrated on the sun rays. Then he began to glow as bright as the sun itself. His arms curdled the glowing rays into the shape of a fireball. Instantly, Daylor threw with all his might the flaming and hot fireballs at the angels. But it had no effect on the angels at all. They threw it back at him by taking their swords and holding it up as a shield so the hot fireballs would reflect and bounce back to him. Daylor decided to split the city of Nirvana in half by gravitational pull. The archangels and Gabriel used the breath of destruction and blew Daylor and his men down towards the earth. Straight into the Realm Of Hell!! Being blown into the Realm Of Hell was a great punishment from the angels. The force of the winds are strong! Sometimes, your bones would break from the hard impact of the strong winds.

There was also powerful and very high lightning and thunder which would make you jump out of your skin. A person is lucky if they escaped the electrical volts of the dangerous lightning. "I will get you for this!" screamed Daylor as he was falling down, down, down into hell. You have not seen the last of me! The city of Nirvana is doomed!! When I return, I will not have no mercy or sympathy on nobody. All of you will wish you had of bowed down to me!"

Chapter Two

Meanwhile, the Supreme Being of the Universe was sitting in his glory. This scene took place in the highest heavens of the heavenly realms. A great cloud surrounded by glittering stars, lightning, thundering, and lots of mists, fire, and wind, surrounded his presence. He observed the corruption of the city of Nirvana and earth. The time structure was not balanced with the earth's axis. He also noticed all earth's problems had been caused by one of the heavenly beings who used to be one of their own. The Supreme Being called a special meeting of urgency. "My heavenly disciples of Nirvana. There is a great evil upon the earth and the city of Nirvana." (While speaking, the Supreme Being shows flashbacks of the earth's turmoil) "One of our fellow beings has decided to take upon himself for his own selfish reasons to steal and read the sacred scrolls and documents of Nirvana, knowing it is against the rules to touch or even read what is written for our specially chosen priests. By doing this, he has turned evil, and even to his appearance now will become hideous and very ugly. There were ancient formulas and spells used by our priests many years ago in these sacred scrolls and documents. He has used these old secrets to become very powerful and dangerous. Our use to be fellow being Daylor even has supernatural strength and powers, and is now using this power for wickedness and destruction for all mankind. Since he has been cast down from the city of Nirvana along with his followers who used to be members of our congregation also, and disobeyed the sacred laws of Nirvana, and became evil, he can no longer use the birth name given to him by the holy monks Daylor no more. Instead, the name of Tribor will be given to him. My fighting angels Gabriel and his archangels has also cast him down into the Realm Of Hell along with his followers. All of them will continue to dwell in darkness for eternity. For they have chosen the dark side. And they will never be allowed again into the holy cities of Nirvana. Everyone on this face of the earth and Nirvana has been plagued by their wickedness. We must put a stop to him and his very wicked organization before the Fullest Blue Moon appears in the earth's solar system. We as Nirvanians, must save innocent people from being destroyed on the earth." This is my plan...

The Realm Of Hell was a very dark and smelly place. Thorny and skeletal. The dwelling of Tribor. There were large cracks on the floor, dead corpses, bats, and so much chaos everywhere. A large throne with skeletal crossbones which was bronzed on each side of his throne was his reigning glory. Even wicked and evil spirits of the dead paid tribute to him. Tribor enters his quarters with each member dancing and chanting his name. Tribor! Tribor! Master of eternal evil and darkness. We worship you! Tribor removes his black hood, revealing his gruesome and scarred face. He once was a beautiful angel, but his evilness converted him to look ugly. And now he even had a black heart. The memories of the teachings and religious statutes of the city of Nirvana had left from him. It was too late to turn back.

Darkness and hell would be his punishment for his betrayal of the gods. Tribor's meeting begins. "My subjects! We have conquered most of the earth. That's good! But to complete our victorious conquest over the earth, we must find the prism stone of Nirvana." This was a heirloom which was passed on from generation to generations of the highest priests of Nirvana. To own or have this precious gemstone in your possession is a great honor. The owner himself of this gemstone would have magical powers, and conquer the entire world. "We must find the prism stone of Nirvana before the Fullest Blue Moon enters it's last rotation phase around the earth. By combining this prism gemstone with my powers, I will become the Supreme Being of the world and the holy city of Nirvana!" Ha! Ha! Ha! But there is one bad obstacle which is standing in my way. He is dwelling on the earth. We must find him quickly before the heavenly beings finds him and tells him of his great powers. He must be stopped! Even if it means his death! And don't fail me! For if you do, it will be your last failure!!! I will surely kill you! Heed my words!!"

Meanwhile the Supreme Being sends different Buddha gods to fly all over the earth to locate the right warriors to conquer over Tribor. This search must be done with spirit and truth. It had to be the right person who would fit the shoes of a Buddha god. Each Buddha god looked into every mortal man and woman's heart and soul. There was not one person who did not get scanned and screened by the Buddha's light of purity and truth. The search was not very long.

When their search was over, eight warriors were very, very, carefully selected. The Buddha gods all came to a final agreement of the specially chosen selected, which also had to be approved by the Supreme Being. They were Chan (Phillipians), Ming (Shaolin Temple China), Michael (Europe Norway), Chaka (Africa), Midori (Japan), Cheyenne (United States), Jade (South America) Raseen (India). After the approval of the Supreme

Being, the chosen warriors were zapped to a specific location for training and instruction. This place of training is called Crystal Mountain. Crystal Mountain was no ordinary Mountain. It's environment consisted of strong Buddha incense, which juggled the senses of your nose once you entered the mountain. An altar neatly displayed different fruits, along with golden candles, a butsudan box made of the finest oak, which was engraved with pure golden designs on it. Fresh green leaves surrounded the altar. The special artifacts placed on the altar such as the rice cup, incense holder, lotus flower symbol, and water cup, were made of pure gold and adorned with red rubies. Other Buddha monks were there, chanting and giving praises to Buddha. At the special meeting place, another Buddha god from Shaolin appears from above. A very sacred ceremony took place. Each person was sworn in. After the initiation, their old clothing magically changed to warrior combat clothing. They also had I-Ching symbols on their arms. The Abbott gives each warrior their own special weapon. Each realm was explained to them. There were ten. "You must collect symbolic items to unlock each realm, said the Abbott. Your goal is to destroy Tribor and make sure he doesn't find the prism stone of Nirvana before the Fullest Blue Moon appears in the earth's solar system." Six special keys were given to Chan who was chosen as the leading warrior.

After closing the ceremony, the Abbott zaps the warriors to a mountainous desert, leading to the door of the Realm Of Anger. They noticed a symbol from the Crystal Mountain, the same place they received their training from. Chan, who had the special keys, took one of the keys and placed it on the special symbol. The door began to open. They all proceeded down inside the dark and dusty realm. The only light the warriors had going down the realm was the torch lights along the walls. As the warriors found their way to the bottom of the stairs, the odor became worse and unbreathable. Michael said, "What is that terrible odor? I can hardly breathe?" "It's making me sick to my stomach!" Chaka said. Sharp piercing screams and heavy thumping noises began to fill the room. "What was that? Jade said. Maybe it's an earthquake! Let's get out of here!"

When all of the warriors came to the center of the caveroom, ugly tazmaian creatures began surrounding them and attacking them. What a surprise attack!

"Who are these creatures?" yelled Chaka out loud to the other warriors.

The creatures of Anger had a very bad foul odor. Their hair was very, very long and shaggy. All of the creatures had their clothes ripped with holes which was also very dusty and smelly. The creepy tazmaians had long rigged fingernails with electrical currents coming from their rusty nails that glowed a sinister dark red. More terrifying creatures as horrible looking as the first appeared. They attacked the shocked warriors in all directions, confusing them. Midori cried out. "It's time to get rid of these smelly creatures once and for all! If we don't defend ourselves now, we will all be killed!" She pulled out her Tai Chi sword, and fought back with all of her strength. "Yeah, you are so right about that! Raseen replied back to Midori. There is so much my nose can take!" Every taz creature continued to make more screeching and howling noises. The warriors noticed the more they fought with them, the more they were led deeper into the cave. Thrashing and slashing with every weapon and skills they could use, the tiredless warriors killed off the tazmaians one by one. Only a few were left. All of a sudden, Chan turned around and said quickly to them, "Stop fighting! Hold your weapons!" Slowly but surely, the smelly creatures of Anger started to leave, one by one. "This is what they want us to do, said Chan. They want us to get so angry, that we would lose track of our senses and time. And this will even delay us more from finding Tribor and the Realm Of Hell. The more we fight, the more deadly and horrifying creatures will appear. This is why they left, because we caught on to their game. You all have done well."

Now it was time to find the door to the next realm. But where was it? The warriors began to search everywhere. Luck was not with them at this time. Suddenly, when Cheyenne slowly walked along the wall on the right side, of a particular spot in the cave, a shiny golden object caught his eyes. He moved very quickly towards it. It was very dusty and filled with grime. Cheyenne anxiously wiped it off. The more he wiped, the more the object became cleaner. When all of the dust was wiped clean, a golden door was revealed. "Look! I think I've found something big here! Cheyenne yelled to his companions. Pointing to the door, he motioned for his companions to come closer to see what he was talking about. Engraved on the door also was a golden lotus flower symbol with two small golden cranes on each side of it. Chan walked up to the door and inserted one of his special keys in the door knob and immediately the golden cranes were released from the lotus flower symbol.

Remembering the instructions of the Abbott, Chan took the cranes. At that moment, all the warriors proceeded into the world of the Realm Of Animality. This realm was enough to scare anybody. This is a place where you hope you could come out alive and tell someone about it.

Inside the Realm Of Animality, there were dangerous black vulgar looking bats, red venomous fire dragons, man eating tigers, poisonous snakes, and deadly reptiles. They were ready and starving to attack their prey, for they were very hungry for flesh and fresh blood. It has been centuries since someone has entered their domain. And whoever did, was certainly doomed! The attack was quick! Every single warrior was fighting madly for their lives. Chaka was occupied with a fierce fire dragon biting at her flesh, while Ming was fighting a fierce deadly tiger. Some of the fighters were badly injured. Blood had gushed everywhere.

But Chaka just like the others, continued to fight. She had to try to kill this mad dragon because she needed his claws for her own personal use. But eventually, with their superb martial arts skills and weapons, the warriors had defeated the monstrous creatures of Animality.

The worn out fighters left from the Realm Of Animality. They finally came to a path where they came upon a golden and green tree with yellow golden bananas hanging from its branches. This was the Realm Of Mystery & Deceit. Above the tree sat a unique prayer wheel. The prayer wheel bought good luck and fortune to anyone who owned it. There were gemstones all over the prayer wheel. Rich in color. And each jewel was very precious and valuable. All the warriors surrounded the gold and green tree. They were very amazed, and had spotted the beautiful and ancient prayer wheel with its magnificent gemstones engraved on it. "How exquisite! said Raseen. This would make a great souvenir for my hobby collection!"

Mysteriously, a brown and yellow monkey appeared when Raseen touched the tree. The very mischievous monkey said to them, "You must solve my riddle! For if you don't solve my riddle, all of you will be forbidden to leave my place."

The strange monkey started laughing and cackling, and jumping around crazily at the same time. "Now here's my riddle! What spiritual food is needed to gain enlightenment?" Each warrior tried to guess the answer to the riddle.

Michael thought quickly and yelled out, "Food! That's the answer!" Ming said to Michael, "You are always thinking of food. No, no. The correct answer is meditation! Ha! Ha!

Ming shouted, "I guessed right! All of you are wrong. The answer is chanting to the Buddha of enlightenment." Midori and Jade began to get frustrated with all the yelling and shouting. Only Chan guessed what the solution to the riddle was. Chan said, "You are all right, but the brown and yellow monkey is looking for a specific answer. It is a very tricky question! I know the right answer. It's simple. Prayer. That's a spiritual food that everyone needs including me. It doesn't have anything to do with the food we eat, or chanting to the Buddha of Enlightenment, or deep meditation." The mischievous monkey realized he was outdone. This Chan, he thought, was wise and had good knowledge. There were two short whistles blown. This was the signal. Quickly, a bunch of other monkeys just like him started to surround the warriors. The monkey gave his sharp command. "Attack all of them!! And kill them!! Let no one here escape alive!!" What a fight it was! It was brutal and bloody. These monkeys had excellent martial arts technique.

Even though the monkeys displayed power and great strength they still were no match for the warriors. Eventually, the monkeys retreated because deep down inside they knew they had lost the fight. These men were very good. And their martial arts, were excellent also. Without wasting any time, Chan quickly climbed up the tree. From branch to branch, he climbed until he reached the very top of the tree, and grabbed the precious prayer wheel there in its glory. It mysteriously glowed when Chan picked it up. At that same time a dark black mist appears out of nowhere. The black mist blinded Chan and his warriors. It was one of Tribor's fearful and deadly men of the lower underworld, Black Skull, who changed himself into the mystical dark mist. During that time, when the fighters were standing around watching Chan climbed the tree, Black Skull switched the female warrior Midori with an imposter named Sefra, a vampire witch, who looked exactly like Midori. She could pass for her twin. Then one of the cranes and prayer wheel, vanishes into thin air as well. Jade started screaming, because the black mist was so strong, it began to strangle her. All of a sudden, the dark mist disappeared. "Look! said Chan. The prayer wheel has been taking right out of my hands! And one of the cranes were taken as well!"

Chapter Three

"It must be the dirty works of Tribor!" There must be something you can do!" said Ming. "That's right, Michael chimed in. I am so surprised he didn't take the keys!" Must be a good, good reason for that!"

"How did Tribor know about these realms? And which one are we at?" Raseen said excitedly. "Then one of you must be a spy! Cheyenne said. How do we know it's not you Raseen!" Raseen looked puzzled by Cheyenne's statement.

Midori (the witch imposter) tried to keep the warriors from getting suspicious. So, she said very sneakly and cleverly, "Why don't we just try to find the next realm." Chan pulled out one of the golden keys from his pocket, and placed it inside the front of an invisible keyhole which only he could see. "How could he do that!" Michael said to himself. I didn't see a thing. Must be magic!" The entrance appeared, and they all jumped into a blue mist which landed them in the Realm Of Hunger.

Inside the third Realm Of Hunger, was a beautiful and mystical botanical paradise garden. There were lovely forest leafy green trees of all colors and origins. Even though this realm was a paradise garden, it was a dangerous and deceptive to the eye. Each branch on every tree bored their own tropical fruits. But one bite, just one bite of these appetizing and tasteful fruits were highly poisonous, and instant death came upon the innocent victim who ate them. These fruits weren't the only attraction on the leafy branches. Gold and silver coins, sparkling jewels, and shiny crystals were also glowing from every tree branch. And underneath each tree, there were treasure chests filled with precious diamonds, pearls, emeralds, sapphires, etc. Michael became overwhelmed with what he saw. And greed begins to settle in his mind. He starts to think very, very sinisterly. So, he plots and schemes on how he could delay the warriors from finding the next realm, because he plans on stealing some of the treasures for himself. "You know what? Michael said suspiciously. We all have been working so hard! Why don't we take some of these precious and lovely jewels for ourselves! It's not going to hurt anybody. And nobody is going to notice who took it. After all, we are the ones who are getting our butts kicked around here. We deserve it!" Ming said, "You know Michael, all of that training and hard work we have been through, and all you think about is money and jewelry. That is definitely a sign of greed. We have an important and dangerous mission to finish. This is our only goal and purpose. And this is not the time to be thinking of only worldly goods, when our lives, and our city, and the earth is at stake. Remember, the Buddha god from Shaolin said we are only allowed to take what is being collected for the mission." Michael said very nasty to Ming, "Finders, keepers, losers weeper. I find, so I keep!" So Michael starts to fill his pouch with some of the jewels. But one of the jewels he picked up, which was the black onyx gemstone, possessed him. An evil and deadly spirit was within the stone. Michael began to change. He started acting very, very violently with the other warriors. His face turned green and hideous. Michael let out a violent and piercing scream. "AAA-HHHHH! AAA-HHH!" His fingernails turned into hugh claws. He developed tremendous strength, and flying abilities. The attack he made upon the warriors came as a surprise to them.

"Turn back now or face death! You cannot win you pitiful mortals of man! screeched Michael. Tribor's sorcery is too strong for you!" Midori, (the witch imposter), stabs him in the heart with her Tai Chi sword. She does this to keep the others from being suspicious of her. Pools of blood splurts out from every part of Michael's body. Then he starts to slowly disintegrate with his flesh falling off his skin. All that remained was a pile of skeletal bones in a pile of dust. Suddenly, one of the fighters, Chaka, notices a red ruby breastplate with an engraved seal of skeletal black crossbones and viper serpents, which symbolizes strength and power, was hanging from one of the trees. Chaka went to grab the red ruby breastplate. Immediately, a dark black mist appeared again. The deadly and mysterious mist was very thick. It choked Chaka so severely, she began to strangle and gag. This is the work of the evil and treacherous work of Black Skull. The red ruby breastplate was stolen right before her eyes. "I cannot believe this is happening! screamed Chaka. One of you has got to be working with that sinister manaic Tribor! The question is, which one of you is it?"

They kept searching for their way out of the realm. But it was so hard to find the way out. There were a lot of paths and trails that led to nowhere. The warriors came to a big river along one of the paths. But there were strange and odd noises coming from somewhere. Each warrior looked at one another. "Well I'm thirsty! said Raseen. Let's drink some of this water from that river." "Wait! said Chan. Let me check it out first." As soon as Chan stretched his hands out over the water, a giant red lobster grabbed for his hands. Chan tried with all his might to fight back.

He tried to reach as best as he could to get to his fighting sword in his back pocket. The other warriors gasped. They tried to hold Chan back to keep him from being pulled inside the deep river waters. Cheyenne acted instantly and pulled the long sword from Chan's pocket, and gave it to him. With one swoosh, Chan cut off the huge lobster's giant claws. It fell back into the river. "Wow!! What a close call!" said each warrior almost at the same time. "It's a good thing you decided to check out the water before we did," said Cheyenne.

"We almost like to been his dinner!" "Let's walk up ahead a little more further, said Chan. Maybe we will come across some fresh water there."

So Chan and his companions walked deep into the forest. Still, not having any knowledge of where they were going or where the path would lead them to. At that moment a sharp twang, like the sound from an arrow caught their attention.

"Look out!" screamed Midori. All the warriors jumped out the way just in time to keep from being hit by an arrow which had electrical currents flowing through it. The electrical arrow hit one of the trees nearby, and the whole entire tree burst into flames. A hideous cackling sound was coming from one of the trees above. As a matter of fact, a couple of cackling laughs. But when the warriors looked up and around, there was no one to be seen. Two more hurling arrows were shot at the warriors coming at tremendous speed.

Each one seemed faster than the other one. “They are trying to kill us! Chaka yelled angrily. And we can’t even see who it is! They must be invisible!” “Look above those orange grove trees, said Cheyenne. I thought I saw something! First it was there, then it wasn’t!” Chan took out his crystal glazer and scanned among the trees. Just above the orange grove trees were perched black witches. Their appearance was horrible! They had on long black robes. Their eyes glowed an eerie fiery red. Every fingernail was very long. So long the nails curved under. The hair was white as the snow, and very long and stringy. On top of their hair was deadly and poisonous asps ready to strike their enemies. Not only did they have one head, but two heads! Chan took some blue mystic powder dust from his pouch, and blew towards the direction of the witches. The blue dust uncovered their invisibility. All the warriors could see them now. “Run!! Run!! screamed Chaka. Run for your lives!!” The wicked witches started flying and chasing them through the forest, throwing swords at them. Swords were being thrown left and right. Swiftly, Chan turned around and threw back sai's at them. Chaka threw fierce fireballs at the witches. "EEEE!! EEEE!!" Screeched the black witches. The mighty forces of Chan's sai's and Chaka's fireballs hit them with tremendous force. Some were killed. The hideous witches disappeared out of sight. "Boy! What a close call!" Chan said.

They kept searching for their way out of the realm. But it was very hard to find their way out. After searching, for what seemed like hours, they came upon a sacred altar of fruits and flowers. Incense filled the air with the sweet fragance Patchouli. Chan, with the golden key, offered it to the altar, and gave three joss incense sticks as an offering. He bowed three times to the altar, and ranged the bell. The two doors to the altar opens wide. Wide enough for the warriors to go through. This is the only way to get to the realm. And each person proceeded into the wide door entrance which led them into the next realm.

Chapter Four

Meanwhile, back in the Realm Of Hell, Tribor is awaiting word from his evil men what the warriors are up to. The vicious and treacherous Black Skull returns with good news.

He pushes all of his loyal followers out of his way. And he insisted on seeing Tribor himself. All of this excitement attracts Tribor's attention. Tribor summons for the dark and gory black mist. "Sire, I came to give a full report on the whereabouts of the warriors, and our undercover Sefra." Tribor said, "That is good! Continue!" With a sneaky and sneering grin, Black Skull tells Tribor how the warriors passed the three realms with much success. Tribor got very angry. "And you didn't try to stop them? roared Tribor. For this you shall die, and lose your life!!" "No! No!" Black Skull howled. He was very, very, afraid of Tribor. Thinking fast and cleverly, he told his master valuable information which he knew could be of great importance to him, and save his neck as well. "I have some items of great value to you. A red ruby breastplate of power. It's gemstones are worth a fortune. I have stolen the sacred prayer wheel, and one of the golden cranes. They are powerless without these precious amulets." "You have done extremely well!" said Tribor. Tribor grabs the stolen amulets from Black Skull, and sends him back with full instructions on how to defeat, stop, and capture the warriors from totally accomplishing their mission. Tribor thinks to himself. "If the first plan I gave to Black Skull does not work out, then I must try another method to hold them back! The time is almost near, for the Fullest Blue Moon to come upon us. Maybe I should work on their weak spot." One of Tribor's evil guardsmen Zador enters. "Sire, one of the female warriors named Midori has been captured and is placed in the dungeon." Sefra, the imposter has replaced her. What shall we do with her? She refuses to give any information about Chan and the others. Should we torture her sire? Or throw her body to the flesh eating lava monsters!" With a rage of fire coming from his mouth Tribor screamed. "Torture her!! Beat her!! Make her talk!! But don't kill her!! We need her!! She will be of great asset to us!! Ha! Ha! Ha!"

The dungeon of Hell was a place where no man on earth would ever want to be. Nor any woman. Darkness and death filled the atmosphere. No sunlight ever penetrated the dark and gloomy dungeon. Midori fought for her life. But she was outnumbered. Not by number, but only by size and strength.

Scorpus, (Tribor's most deadliest and dangerous head guards-men) knew Midori was very powerful and very skillful with her martial arts, so he used one of his deadly sting claws to knock her out unconscious. "Say goodnight, Midori."

Scorpus grabs her violently, throws her to the floor, and stings her with an injection of his deadly poison. Then he flings her lifeless body into the dark and dusty cell. "Make sure she gives you all the information about each warrior, instructed Scorpus to the regular guardsman. Their true identities. The secret to their powers, and who is the specially chosen warrior that has been sent to destroy Tribor. Continue to torture her! But make sure she does not die! Tribor still wants her alive. I have not injected her with a full dosage of my highly intoxicated poison." "Okay Scorpus," said the dungeon guardsman."

Meanwhile, the tired and hungry and wounded warriors entered the Realm Of Humanity. Chan stopped for a moment to take a look at his sutra book which contained vital and graphic pictures of each realm, and the order they each should be in. He read out loud to them the passages in the book. Each one is wondering why the realms are not in order. They had the strictest counseling and instructions taught to them from the beginning.

And they were told each realm would be in order. Ming begins to chant the religious chant which was taught to him by the Abbott. Nam-Myoho-Renge-Kyo, Nam-Myoho-Renge-Kyo, Nam-Myoho-Renge-Kyo, to receive help and guidance from the Buddha gods. Chan starts to read the ancient sutra book of the Buddha gods again, so he could get a clear perspective of why these realms are not in exact order. Reading a sutra book can give some kind of pure enlightenment to your mind of why things are not happening according to the prophecies and regulations of the Buddha gods. After the reading, each of the fighters go their own separate ways. Jade and Chaka went to search for food, water, and possibly for any type of healing herbs. Raseen is complaining. "I am sick and tired of this! We have been talking and also been attacked by strange monkeys. There have been man eating animals and ugly creatures ready to have us for lunch and dessert. A giant lobster tried to kill Chan. We all had been running for our lives and shot at with arrows and God knows whatever by black witches. Let me see, what else. Oh yes. One of our men got possessed and turned green. And this dam black mist, keeps tracking us down to find out how we are doing. So you mean to tell me we should be brave and act like this is not nothing? I don't know about the rest of you, but I am leaving. Good bye! I leave these creatures and the rest of the realms to you."

Midori, (the evil imposter) said, "Why don't you relax, and take it easy." Chan said, "She is right. There has to be a solution to all this. Look at the sky. The blue moon is almost at its fullest phase. Have you noticed things aren't the same as they should be? This is not the time to lose your faith and courage. Remember, we also are being tested."

"All of us must be strong! We were chosen for a reason." Two hours went by. Everyone of the fighters agreed with one another. Suddenly, a huge gust of wind starts to blow slowly and swiftly. White clouds and a vapor mist appeared. There were no chances being taken. Each one placed their hands on their weapons. When the white clouds and mist disappeared, there stood the Buddha goddess of mercy and compassion, Kuan Yin. She was so beautiful and lovely, that even when she spoke, her words would melt into your mind and heart. The apparition of this goddess was also very stunning. This goddess of beauty had long flowing shiny black hair. A lotus flower embroidered the top of her head adoringly. And the golden white halo which glowed above her, encircled her long and shiny black hair. She wore a white silk and silver flowing gown embedded with diamond studs on it. Imprinted on the breast part of the gown was the lotus flower symbol.

Her gold bracelets were worn on her left hand, that were made from genuine lotus beads. Held in her hand very dearly laid Buddhist prayer beads. Each bead had been made of pure crystal quartz. Hanging on her neck were draped sparkling diamond necklaces. She sat so very lovingly upon a lotus flower bed. "My name is Kuan Yin. I am the goddess of mercy and compassion."

Encouragement and instructions was given to the warriors. Food was given as well. Also, herbal medicines for healing had been given to the worn out fighters to heal them mentally, physically, and spiritually. Kuan Yin spoke to them very softly. "The last three realms are going to be your biggest challenges. This will test your faith, power, and courage. But beware! There are traitors among you! I cannot reveal this to you, for you have to find this out for yourselves. This is the part where you will have to use your keen sense of perception. May Buddha be with you."

Raseen blurted out, "I knew it! You cannot fool me about this!" Kuan Yin compresses her two hands together and opens her hands like a book. A radiant spiral violet flame swirled around her hands, and encircled the warriors. (All except the warrior imposter Midori, who is really Sefra, the accomplice of Tribor). The brave fighters were so excited about receiving this special blessing from Kuan Yin, that they didn't notice the violet flame did not encircle around the fake Midori. Then she pointed to them in a vision the path of endurance which leads to the three mountains. Kuan Yin explains. "Beyond the three mountains of the Red Dragon Mountain, Mystic Mountain, and Ninja Mountain, you will find the door that leads to a Buddhasavatta. Remember, all is not what it seems. There is a lot of danger. You have only three days to complete your mission. Use your powers you were trained for, and use them wisely." Turning her head to Chan, Kuan Yin advises Chan because he is the head leader and he needed to be give special instructions. "Use the elements around you. Always motivate yourself in the arts, and draw all your internal and external power from the flowing waters of the Dragon's Gate." Kuan Yin vanishes into thin air. Chan looks puzzled by her words. Following the path which leads to the three mountains, the fighters came upon a large hill which had a tremendous height. Chan chanted a few magical words upon the warriors, and they immediately had the power to fly up the large hill which would lead them to the entrance of Ninja Mountain. Danger came upon them sooner than it was expected. When they landed at the top of Ninja Mountain, every deadly flying Ninja came from trees, and underneath the ground. The Ninjas began their horrible attack upon the surprised warriors. These Ninjas were not ordinary Ninjas. They had special supernatural powers. Invisibility, superb martial arts skills, and weapons that kill instantly, as well as sorcery and magic, was used without no remorse or guilt.

For they were trained to fight hard, even if it led to their own deaths. Chaka used her laser power from her bracelets to zap the Ninjas. These lazers were so powerful, it could disintegrate anybody within seconds. Chaka did manage to kill off at least four of the Ninjas, but they were so fast and quick that the others from behind her, got a chance to slash her arms and her legs. Red blood started gushing everywhere. Ming placed his hands together in a prayer like position, and began channeling. A high glowing beam of white light, which came from his bare hands, blinded the killer Ninjas. Jade takes her Tai-Chi sword and begins to use the Wushu Stance. She cuts their heads totally off, and their hands, thrashing and slashing with her Tai-Chi sword.

Midori (the evil imposter) was not attacked by the vicious Ninjas because they knew she was one of their kind. Their boss was her boss. The villain and evil master himself, Tribor. Chan used his flaming sword of the Buddha. A strong and deadly weapon also. He charges at them like a jungle lion. And attacks all the Ninjas from left to right.

The fatal and final blow hit the main leader of the Ninjas.

Chan did this by throwing his sword which flew at super speed. The sword started sparkling and hissing with hot lazer charged atoms of electrical red rays, which penetrated directly into the heart of the main Ninja. Raseen, who observed the whole entire fight was amazed at this technique way of fighting. "Incredible! I didn't know you had it in you! said Raseen. Why didn't you use your martial arts skills like that before?" Chan said to Raseen, "I never knew I had these powers! Each time, there is always more and more of these skills I wind up finding out I have."

Raseen gave him a look of approval. "You certainly know it now!! Wooo-ooooo!!"

Chapter Five

When all the other Ninja men that were left realized they had lost the battle, and their leader was fatally killed, the remaining Ninjas retreated and disappeared. Strange and mysteriously the imposter Midori also vanished. Raseen and Ming noticed this. Jade said, "You know, it's very strange, but every time when we are just about to get killed, or get into a fight, Midori always stands to the side of us and do nothing. Notice, none of our enemies attacks at her either.

She is always looking at Chan, and tries to get close up on him. Midori practically guards him all the time. And I really observed this a couple of times, even at the very beginning of Ninja Mountain." "That's very, very, strange indeed!" Cheyenne said. "Chan must have something she wants pretty badly, Chaka said. I wonder what it is? Maybe she has the hots for him. You know, Chan is a good looking guy." Ming turned around and said to Chaka and Cheyenne, "Will you two please stop talking and start flying down this mountain. We don't have time for gossip!"

After a safe landing, the warriors continued to walk along the path to the next mountain on their journey. The path led them into a deserted valley that led into the Realm Of Desertion. After walking a distance, the fighters came upon a tiny village. This village was very old, and runned down, and real dusty. Raseen yelled out loud. "Is there anybody here?" The only sounds they heard were the loud echoes coming from Raseen's voice. Chan began to laugh and said, "I don't think anybody has been here for many centuries. Just look at this place! Must be deserted."

Cheyenne said, "That's why nobody answered you when you yelled. Look! There's another path over there need that dead tree. It might lead us to Mystic Mountain." "Why not?" Ming said to Cheyenne. "That is the only mountain I see ahead of us."

As soon as the warriors began to walk the long dusty path, they sanked deeper and deeper into the sand they were walking on. This sandy path turned out to be quicksand.

"Must be the Realm Of No Return," Chan said to himself.

It was. He takes out his magical rope from the side of his uniform, and throws it so it can loop around one of the branches of a nearby tree. Suddenly, huge quicksand monsters with red beaming eyes, pulled all the warriors back down further into the heavy muddy quicksand. One of the monsters grabbed Chan who was trying so desperately not to let go of his magical rope.

Cheyenne was struggling and gasping for air. Raseen pulled his sword out and started to slash the monsters in half. But amazingly, the quicksand monsters slowly reconnected back together again, piece by piece, right before their eyes. Raseen shouted to Chan hysterically. "Chan! You better start using your special martial arts stuff!! We need you bad now!! Help-pppp!!!"

Raseen began to sink more further, and deeper and deeper into the muddy swamp quicksand water.

Chan quickly took out the precious Nirvana prism stone, and held it in the palm of his nervous hands, pointing it right towards the terrifying quicksand monsters. He didn't even realize this gemstone was in his pouch until he pulled it out. And it was astonishing how he already knew how to use it! "I will check to see what other items are in here, when I get a chance," Chan said to himself. This magical gem was the only source and power that Chan could really depend on to defeat his enemies if all else fails. A giant red and yellow ray of light encircled the muddy, beastly creatures with a lot of force so great, it caused them to screech and howl, and explode boom! into fragments. Then Chan pointed the Nirvana prism stone at each warrior and upon himself.

The bodies of all the warriors, including Chan, levitated out of the swampy quicksand.

Upon arriving at Mystic Mountain, the fighters couldn't find the entrance. Chan who was standing at the site with his men started remembering the oath he took, the special sutra book, and special weapons given to him. Realization came to him. He was the chosen one. He also came to conclusion that the power and skills were already there. But, he had to find this out by himself, or else he wouldn't believe he was the chosen one. Chan, now with even more strength and confidence in himself, chanted boldly with his whole heart and soul. "I call upon the five elements of water, fire, wind, and earth, and wood, to release their flow of spiritual essence of energy and transforming power to reveal the mystic spiral staircase. I respectfully thank you for your mercy and loving kindness." A streak of blue light mixed with fire and crystals appeared and spiraled around the mountain, and a mystical golden yellow staircase glowed before them. The fighting warriors ascended onto the glowing moving escalator steps until they reached the very top of Mystic Mountain. At the top of Mystic Mountain, was a red door with seven golden bolts and a special seal. This was the seal of Hotei. Written on it were oriental symbols.

Chan translated. Realm Of Wisdom And Knowledge. The red door led to inner chamber doors. When the doors opened, each warrior walked inside, afraid, because they did not know what other hidden danger might be upon them. There were different Buddhasattavas exquisite statues hanging on the walls. The hall was long, narrow, and decorated very elegantly, with tiles that shined like gold. Each Buddha statue was dressed in sacred royal attire, deep in meditation. There was a blue altar decorated with holy religious artifacts of jasmine incense, tall yellow tapered candles in bronze candle holders. Yellow and red lotus flowers placed in pure golden and red oriental vases was engraved with the symbols of the lotus flower images on them. Large gold and red goblet cups filled with fruits encircled the yellow blossoming lotus flowers. A large Buddha statue made of pure gold called Hotei, with diamond shaped eyes, made of real genuine diamonds, sat upon the sacred altar. Hotei is sitting in a deep mediation position.

Chan recognizes the Buddha god and it's holy altar. So to give respect to Buddha, he chants a sacred chant. As soon as the chant was over, Chan begins to feel the spirit of the Buddha god. Hotei sends a telepathy message to Chan and appears to him. "Buddha's name be praised. Give me every thing you have collected from the other realms my son. Even if you do not have all of them to give. Your mission will soon be completed, said Hotei. It will be a very hard one.

Your final battle still lies ahead of you at Tribor's kingdom. You must use all of your skills and wisdom and courage to win this mission that you were especially chosen for. I am going to let you keep the Nirvana prism until your mission is finally completed. But remember, do not let this precious gemstone fall in the hands of Tribor. For if you do, all is lost. I will help you and the warriors to get to the evil Tribor's Realm Of Hell. May Buddha be with you." With a wave of his hands, a white spiral light, flashes before them. Hotei said, "Walk through the white spiral light, so you can enter the Dragon's Gate at the waterfall. Be careful! Great danger awaits you!" Hotei vanishes into thin air.

Chapter Six

The dragon's gate is a very large waterfall which is sacred to Asian people. All the warriors had to walk through this giant waterfall to get to the other side of Dragon's Gate. Meanwhile, at the other side waiting for them, were Tribor's vicious and wicked accomplices. Sefra, (still disguised as Midori), and Black Skull and his black skeletal army of men.

Black Skull and his black skeletal men, had plans to attack when they reached the other side of the waterfall at ancient Dragon's Gate.

"We must strike to kill!" Black Skull said to Sefra and his army of darkness. This time there will be no mistakes! Here they come now! Attack! Attack! Have no mercy upon no one!!" The fighting scene was grusome and deadly. So much blood was shed. The clouds in the sky filled the air with total darkness. Strong lightning and thundering clashed with each other violently. The sun was no longer shining its rays of sunlight. Ghosts and evil spirits arose from their gravesites to help with the attack upon Chan and his men. They were screeching and howling with such madness.

The earth trembled violently. The army of Black Skull wore their battle suits of armor. And their swords were very sharp and long. Their shields and swords bore the initial symbol of BS. Black Skull. “Ha!! Ha!! Ha!!” laughed the scrupulous and treacherous Black Skull. He looked around and above him. “Good! Good! All my men are here. Now we can begin the battle. Every fighter of Black Skull, fought with all of their might. His men even used lasso ropes, charged with electricity. Poisoned darts were hurled at Chan and his men. Some of the skeletons did acrobats of jumping, kicking, and cartwheels with super speed. Whosh!! Whosh!!

You can hear the impact sound of the speed. Some of the skeleton men thrusted themselves in front of the warriors.

Little sharp blades zipped out from their long and gory looking skeleton fingers.

But the warriors of Chan were too powerful for Black Skull’s army. They were empowered with even greater skills and more fighting power since Buddha appeared to them. Their hand grenades with spikes on them, blew the skeleton bones to many pieces. Chan even called upon the four winds of the North, South, East, and West to blow the army of darkness far back into the graveyard pits, from which they came. Sefra, Black Skull, and his army of men, knew they had been defeated. “Retreat!! Retreat!” howled Black Skull.

All of his men retreated and vanished puff! right before Chan and his men's eyes.

It was a long and hard trail to the other mountain, Red Dragon Mountain. If you could get pass the venomous cobras, rattlesnakes, and water moccasin snakes, a person would value their life. This was the only path that led to the mountain. Even to the deadly and giant lizards waited for you, for they were hungry and thirsty for food. You are the enemy. In their territory. And you were the hunted. With one large gulp, a giant lizard can swallow you whole. All the men ran for their lives. "Run!! Run!!" screamed Jade. "These creatures are after our blood and our flesh! Raseem said. "Throw some of them spiked grenades at them! That might slow the animals down!" It did.

As they proceeded along the hunted trail, Ming spotted Red Dragon's Mountain up ahead. "Look! We have finally reached Red Dragon's Mountain, and possibly our destiny." When the warriors walked towards the deadly and red rocky mountain, each warrior bounced back onto the ground. There was an invisible force field, shielding the entire mountain. "Oh God! yelled Rasheen. We are doomed! And we have come all this way for nothing! I don't know why we went through all this training, and trial and tribulations.

Now we have failed." "Don't worry, said Chan. This is not the time to give up! We must all have faith. Remember, Hotei is with us!" Chan takes out the Nirvana prism, and his Violet Flame Sword to penetrate through Tribor's invisible force shield.

Chan with all his might, threw his flaming sword towards the force field. The mighty sword cut through the invisible field just as if it was paper. The protective barrier had broken. Chan's Violet Flame Sword, boomeranged back into Chan's hands. And the fiery blue, white, and yellow flame went out.

The men walked through the force field just like magic. It closed back behind them. They instantly flew up high into Red Dragon's Mountain, which has lots of red colored crystal rocks, thorny bushes, poisonous snakes, and vultures. Finally, what seemed like it took a lifetime, everyone made it to the top. There was a huge dark maze. This was the horrifying Realm Of Mazes. All the warriors walked very, very cautiously through the dark and gory maze. Torches had to be lighted. It was a sight no human would want to see.

Everywhere in their path and sight, were rotten smelly corpses lying around, skeletal bones, and half bloody mutilated body parts. Even haunting, screeching, evil spirits surrounded them. The poisonous snakes and vultures came after them as well. Even the thorny bushes came to life and extended their long prickly branches out to sting and scratch up the warriors severely. The more deeper and deeper they ran into the scary maze, the hotter and hotter, it got. The foul and smelly odors became unbearable. There were secret trap doors which if fallen into would lead to their death. Towards the end of the maze, a beautiful green sparkling light shined ahead of them. So, they followed the light. It led them out of the maze. "We've made it out of the maze!!" shouted Chaka. "I am so glad!" Raseen said. "At first, I thought we were so lost we would never find our way out of that monstrous maze!" chimed in Ming.

As the warriors hugged and congratulated themselves, a Buddhist nun appeared from out of nowhere. She sat upright with her prayer beads in her hands with her eyes closed in deep prayer. Situated behind the nun, stood a small and unique monastery. Inside the monastery stood tall and black candles, fresh flowers, copper incense burners, and glass stained windows. The fresh smell of jasmine incense filled the air of the small monastery. This ancient monastery looked exactly like one of the monasteries of the city of Nirvana. Chan and his men passed by the praying nun and went inside the temple. Due to respect, they did not want to disturb her while she was praying. Deep in thought, Chan thought to himself. "I know I have seen a picture of this old monastery before in my sutra book." But why would there be a duplicate so far out this way? And some things are missing. Hm-mm." Everybody looked around and stood in amazement. There were puzzled looks on each and every face.

"Something's not right here, Cheyenne said. I remember Chan showing us in his sutra book, all the pretty monasteries of Nirvana. And each one had it's history written below the picture, including how each monastery was decorated inside.

There are some items missing in here. That's strange! And who is nanny the nun out there." Chan said to Cheyenne, "You are very sharp! I was wondering the same thing." "Gets confusing, doesn't it? said Ming. Why don't we ask the old nun and find out." "Maybe she can give us some of the answers to our questions," blurted out Raseen. The old nun who had finished praying, ignored the expressions on all their faces and tried to encourage and assure them of their safety. "Put down your weapons, the nun said weakly. You are safe here. This is a place of worship for the Buddha god Hotei. No one will bother you here."

The nun begins to light three purple joss sticks she was holding in her bare hands. She also bowed three times.

Chan and the others, starts to get suspicious of the old nun. His vibrations begin to bother him very badly. He remembered distinctively the warnings from the beautiful and loving goddess Kuan Yin. (He flashes back) More and more Chan's psychic vibrations got stronger and stronger that something wasn't right. He noticed a red strange fiery glow in her eyes. Something sinister, something evil. She did have an evil eye. Chan turned around, and scanned the odd monastery behind him. His unique powers gave him the ability to perceive things like x-ray vision. One of the symbols that he saw on the stained glass windows earlier caught his attention. He scanned all the stained windows again. All the symbols on the windows was not one of the sacred Buddha symbols which meant enlightenment and everlasting life. As a matter of fact, it wasn't even similar to the other Buddha symbols at all. Instead, it had the symbols of three moons interlocked together with a signature letter "T" engraved on it. But it was unrevealing to the eyes. Nobody could see it.

Chapter Seven

Chan quickly reaches for the Violet Flame Sword. But he changes his mind, and decided to take out the gemstone prism of Nirvana. The prism glowed brightly, and flickered very furiously. Immediately, the rays for the prism shined everywhere, scanning every inch of the ancient monastery.

It revealed that the monastery was fake and just a mirage!

Then, the prism scanned the old nun. Instantly, a transformation took place. Lo and behold! The old nun turned out to be Komodo! He was disguised as her. Tribor did a magical spell, and turned Komodo into the weakly nun. This lizard dragon called Komodo, is the most wickedest, cunning, killer, man eating dragons of men in the world. And the most highest lord of the dark side, and the commander in chief of his own armies. He was just as powerful as Tribor. They were very good friends. Each one helped one another out. No matter what the situation was. Again, violent thunder and lightning struck the skies above. And a deep dark shadow covered the earth. The ground shook violently.

Rising everywhere, from underneath the ground, arose his army of darkness. The black armies were from every corner of the earth who came out of hell. Past and present, who had been evil and wicked and lost their souls to the dark side had now awaken, and are ready to do their master's bidding. Now that they were awoke, the armies were pre-pared for battle. It had been a very long time since they had an encounter with the enemy. And the smell of fresh flesh was on their minds. This was the time to kill for them. No sympathy or sorrow for the enemy. These army of darkness had cold hearts. If they would have to kill their master, they would do it. And this is exactly why Komodo did not trust any of them. He knew very well how heartless and cruel they could be. But these are the kind of men he wanted. They were just like him.

Komodo was an ugly and hideous dragon reptile creature who stood seven feet tall. He was black and brown and very scaly with sharp black and red beady eyes. Very enormous in size and weight, he could smell things with his twelve foot long pinkish tongue which had a split at the very tip. His tongue was long enough to thrash or grab his enemy at a long distance. His black claws were curved, long, sharp, and pointy, just like the T-Rex dinosaur. One swipe was fatal.

Komodo was a deadly fire-breathing dragon. And his venomous saliva which is filled with highly poisonous bacterial and toxic waste, as well as acid, can kill a victim in a matter of seconds or melt them away to nothing. His saliva is just as dangerous, because like the king of the cobras, he could spit his poisonous venom at long distances as well. He also was a professional in martial arts.

Komodo wore an amulet around his neck. Exactly the same symbol as Tribor's signature ring. Komodo, very proud, arrogant, and nasty, said to the warriors, "You are on my territory! There is no escape for you! All of you quietly surrender now and bow down to me! Do you think you puny warriors with your toy weapons can defeat me? HA! HA! HA!

How foolish! I control your powers now !! I am your master now!! The world belongs to me!! Surrender or die!!" The master dragon gave a loud battle cry. He took his amulet off his neck and tossed it into the sky. It made crackling noises as it rotated. This was the signal for the battle to start. All of his army of swarming dead zombies, flying vampires, evil spirits, demons, and a whole tribe of deadly warriors from hell violently attacked from every direction.

The army swarmed around them like killer bees. "Oh no! Chan gasped to himself. If that darn prism gets into the hands of Komodo, we are in serious trouble!"

It seems there were no escape. Even the flying vampires had teeth like razors, that could tear your flesh apart. They were knawing and biting the warriors, piercing their skins.

Tearing at their flesh. Large clots of blood was dripping from their mangled and torn flesh. The flow of dripping red blood from the warriors bodies increased the flying vampires appetite. For they were hungry and thirsty for blood. The ordinary zombies and army of darkness zombies had deadly powers too. Their lazer eyes could set you on fire, and one squeeze can crush you to death. The army of darkness zombies were special and more deadlier because on top of their heads were poisonous asps, ready to strike out at their victims. Three of the warriors, Chan, Jade, and Cheyenne, were badly hurt. It seemed so impossible to defeat such evil and dangerous forces. Chan still continued to fight. While Chan was fighting with the dragon Lord Komodo, the gemstone prism of Nirvana drops out of his pocket. One of the sinister flying vampires saw the prism gemstone drop out of Chan's pocket and flies to get it. "Ahaa! said the flying vampire. The prism has been dropped!

I have to catch the prism. If I capture it, I know Tribor will ask me to be his queen, and sit on his throne. And we can rule the world forever!!"

Chan and the vamp struggles furiously for the prism. The vamp bites and slashes him with her sharp teeth and nails at Chan's arms and neck.

More blood gushes out. "Why don't you give up the prism? said the vamp to Chan. This is my prism! I know how to use it more than you do! You are dying!!" Hee! Hee! Hee! After a continous struggle, Chan grabs back the prism and holds it in front of the frantic vamp's face. "I cast you back to the realm of darkness where you belong!" The vicious and cackling vamp catches on fire. "So help me Chan, if it's the last thing I do, I will get even with you, no matter how long it takes!!" She begins to vaporize, and disintegrated to ashes. Afraid that his wicked men were defeated, Komodo used his amulet again. This time his amulet made an even louder and higher pitched crackling sound, and rotated ten times faster than before. The fake monastery shook very furiously and began to smoke. There was a loud and big explosion. A fiery rain of hail came down upon the fake monastery. Tribor appears! Tribor was dressed in his combat attire. He wore a black cloak with a hood that covered his face. His breastplate was engraved with his symbol on it.

"Welcome warriors of Nirvana! I have been expecting you for a long time. I am a fair man. All of you know that I, Tribor, am far more superior and much more an expert in the arts than you are! This little match of yours will not be any real competition to me at all! Surrender now! You so called warriors of Nirvana, and maybe, just maybe I will spare your lives!" Ming said, "We will never surrender to you!" Tribor said to the guard, "Bring the prisoner out now! Be prepared to see one of your followers die!!" The guard brings out a prisoner. It was Midori. The real Midori. She was badly tortured and beaten severely. She struggled with the guardsmen screaming and pleading, "Let me go! You ugly piece of slimy slug!!"

Midori tries to warn her friends, "It's a trap! Turn back!

Tribor and his army just want us to fail our mission! Don't be fooled by his devious trickery. His power is failing. And whatever you do, do not give him the prism of Nirvana!"

The guard became angry, and tries to shut Midori up from talking too much, by covering her mouth with his slimy hands. Raseen said, "This female that looks just like Midori cannot be her. She was with us during this whole journey! This is one of Tribor's tricks! I know how he is."

"This character never tells the truth. This is why he hides his face! "No looks!" Chan said. I remember now, she rapidly and quickly disappeared all of a sudden at Ninja Mountain. The Midori who was with us is a fake all along. I realize this now. Have you noticed that nothing ever happened to her?"

Jade said to Chan, "That's the reason why she guarded you so closely, because she knew you had the prism, and I also believe she was the spy for Tribor." Chaka said, "This broad needs to be taught a lesson. She got a lot of nerve trying to spy on someone." Cheyenne said to his companions, "The real Midori must have been held prisoner at Tribor's dungeon and replaced with a fake. That's how Tribor knew our every move. The fake Midori would probably sneak off somewhere unknown to us and communicate with her master Tribor." Midori was thrown harshly to the ground by the guardsmen. She speaks out in distress. "Don't you guys recognize me? Here is my marking." She raises her torn, bloody, and bruised arm up, rips off part of her torn sleeves to reveal the warrior symbol.

A frightening war cry is heard. One of the flying zombies who did not fight with Komodo and the other zombie men at the waterfalls of the Dragon's Gate, came from behind her and squeezes her to death. Her spirit leaves from her body.

This means that her spirit had become separated from her frail body. Her body gives off a glittering white diamond glow and quickly vanishes into the air. This is too much to bare. All of her friends cried out her name. "Midori! Midori! We will always love you!" Cheyenne, Ming, Chaka, Raseen, Jade, and Chan, began to attack Tribor and Komodo.

They were upset their faithful friend had died right before their eyes. This was a sad time for them all. And everyone would miss her very much.

Chapter Eight

Tribor, afraid that Chan and his men will catch on to his schemes, carried out his second plan. For he was a shrewd person who always was clever and crafty, and ahead of the game. With one wave of Tribor's hand, all of the warriors flew in different directions, because of his great force of power. A red sonic laser beam came out from Tribor's eyes, striking at every warrior. The impact was so great, the earth split open, and Chan fell deep into it. He was knocked out on conscious. Blood spilling from the side of his forehead. The rest of them were sent back to the last realm, where the fake monastery was located at. Raseen looked around, and noticed they were back at the monastery.

"Isn't this a trip? yelled Raseen. Here we are back at this old monastery. It's nothing but pieces now. And what ever happened to Chan? Knowing Tribor, he closed the time zone so we cannot get back to where we were!" said Raseen. Cheyenne said to Raseen and the others, "You know Chan has the prism, so we have to get back to him."

They walked around the condemned old monastery to look for clues to get out. Ming was trying to figure out how they all got there. "Does anybody know what kind of sorcery Tribor used?"

Ming said. Chaka said, "You know it was an evil spell. We haven't graduated to that yet!" You guys, I think we should put our minds together and try to figure out what kind of place this is. I know for a fact, that this is also an illusion." Jade said to them humbly, "Let's look for a secret door that can get us out of here." Raseen said, "Jade, I hate to burst your bubbles, but, have you noticed that this place was destroyed to ashes!! I really would like to see any door survive that explosion. That would be a super door alright!" "Raseen, would you please stop being so critical and try to find something?" said Jade.

"Well I am highly insulted!" Raseen spoke back to her. "Stop talking, and look, the both of you, said Cheyenne. Chan is going to need us."

All of them proceeded to look through the rubble and ashes that had been left behind in the explosion. "Did anybody find anything?" yelled Chaka. "Keep on searching, we will find something!" called out Ming. Ming suddenly noticed a brown piece of marble sticking out of the mangled burned wood. He began to remove more of the wood. The more wood he removed, the more it looked like a secret passage. "I think I found something! shouted Ming. Maybe this will take us back to where Chan is." Raseen torted, "I don't like it! Noop! I don't like it at all! You don't know where this leads to." "I don't remember when we had our sutra books while we were at training, that a hidden passage was located here," said Chaka. Cheyenne said to them pointing down to the direction of the hidden passage, "Right now we do not have a choice. Let's go." Raseen went first. The remaining fighters proceeded down behind him. After a few minutes of climbing down, Raseen was beginning to get tired of so many stairs. He turned to them and said, "You know what? This is taking too long! I am going to fly down." "I can't believe he's finally going ahead of somebody," Jade said. Chaka agrees. "He needs to be scared more often."

The secret passage was very deep down inside. Raseen thought, "How long I have to keep flying down? Is there a bottom?" No sooner than he said this, he hit the bottom with a hard bang. "Well, I've found the bottom!" Little did Raseen know, he had company. Bad company. The others flew right behind him. They walked through the passage very carefully. Not knowing what lied ahead. "Didn't you see a pair of eyes staring at us?" Raseen said. "What eyes?" Cheyenne said. "There he goes again! Jade said to Chaka.

I knew his bravery wasn't going to last." Just at that moment, a loud growl was heard. Cheyenne said, "What was that?" From out of nowhere a big wild cat, with orange and black spots, leaped at Cheyenne. The huge beast roared and growled again. Ming said to the fighters "Look! Here comes the rest of them!" The wild cats were savages. The queen was the leader of her pack. She stood behind, watching and observing the fight. Their sharp and long claws were ready to strike. Ming shouted, "This is a fine mess Raseen got us in! He flew down too far!" Raseen said, "You worry too much!" "I will save all of you!" Everyone said at the same time, "And what can you do?" Jade said, "Yeah! He almost flunked training." Raseen pulled out the Dragon Head Sword with much difficulty. He kept tugging, but it wouldn't unlock from its blade case. Chaka said, "Some hero! I rather be lost in the wilderness!" Finally, the blade released itself from its case. When the wild cats attacked, Raseen, with his eyes closed, slashed the untamed animals. He slashed left and right, killing them. All the fighters were shocked and amazed at how Raseen killed off the animals. "Great job! Ming said. I didn't know you had it in you!" Raseen who was sweating profusely said, "I didn't know I had it in me either!"

But all was not over with. For there lurking on the side in the dark was the queen of the wild cats!

She looked ready to kill with her red fierce eyes. "How dare you come into my domain and kill off my precious cats!! If you had any misunderstandings with Tribor, that's your problem! The question is, now what should I do with you all? Have you all for a nice dinner? Or give you people back to Tribor?"

The warriors looked at one another. They could not believe she was talking! "What's the matter? You think us cats cannot talk! We are highly intelligent! Now be prepared to die!" The queen of cats did somersaults and flips. She was ready to attack her enemies. Raseen held on to his sword. "I'm not afraid of you, you sassy pussycat!" "My strength is just as great as yours! screeched the wild cat queen. Die warriors!! Die!!" At that second, the queen wild cat jumped upon Raseen. With all his might, he thrust the keen Dragon Head Sword into the heart of the beast. She fell down dead.

After the vicious fight was over, Raseen and his companions decided to call for help. They said a special chant to Kuan Yin. She came to their rescue without hesitation. "I knew you would come! Raseen said to her. We feel safe now! But we all were separated from Chan. Can you send us back to the same place where Chan was?" Kuan Yin the goddess of compassion spoke. "You all have done so well. I am so proud of you. And yes, I will send you and the fighters back to where Chan was last." Her white mist fills the whole place. The warriors start feeling strange. When the mist goes away, they find themselves at the last place where they fought. They started an extensive search for Chan, calling out his name. "Chan! Chan! Where are you? Answer us!"

Chapter Nine

Meanwhile, Chan who had been trapped and unconscious, began to wake up. "OOH! My head! he said. How did I get here?"

He heard loud voices calling out his name. As best as he could, he yelled and screamed as loud as he could, "Over here!! I'm over here!!" Raseen, Chaka, Ming, Cheyenne, Jade, followed his voice and flew to his location. "Over here!! Over here!!" Chan shouted again. Look down!!" "Look! Chaka said. There's a hugh crack in the earth over there!

He could be stuck! Let's look!" Sure enough, there was Chan. "Let's pull him out!" Chaka said. She reached for her magical lasso. Chaka flung it at Chan down below. The mystic lasso wrapped itself around Chan's entire body and pulled him out. Chan looked in a daze. He was badly hurt.

Cheyenne said to Chan, "Take out your prism! It's the only thing that can save your life and heal you!" Chan weakly reached for his pouch and searched for the prism. It was not there! Ming said, "Did you drop it somewhere?" "I don't think so, Chan said to him. It should be in here!"

Jade also said to Chan, "Do you remember the last time you used the gemstone?" "Who knows? Chan answered back to her.

But I do know that it was here in my pouch. I think someone came when I was thrown into this pit, and took it from me. But who?"

"That's just great! You know what? I am really sick and tired of this mission. Do you remember when we all was in training, what did our teacher said? Practice, practice, practice. And that very famous saying, have faith, said Cheyenne. The teachers, the training, and the sutras did not tell us about this kind of evil." "Calm down! Cheyenne. All is not lost. We are still here and should thank the Buddha gods that we have our lives," said Ming. Cheyenne said, "I don't want to sound ungrateful, but this did not help Midori, didn't it! She is dead and won't be able to fight anymore. And what about Michael. We don't even know where he is, or what has happened to him." "Cheyenne, this is not the time to lose your cool. Right now, at this very moment, we must pull ourselves together, Chan said. "You know something else? I am also sick and tired of this. One way or another I will find the gemstone myself and end this evil menace once and for all!"

Cheyenne begins to fly away from the fighters. "Cheyenne! Cheyenne! Come back! You don't know whats out there!" yelled Jade. Chan gave a direct order. "One of you follow him. He might get into some unknown danger. You cannot fight these demons in this place alone." Jade begins to fly away. Chaka said to Chan, "This is Tribor's strategy. If we are altogether, he knows it will be very hard to defeat us. But if he separates us, Tribor knows he will have a better chance and victory. I hope Jade finds Cheyenne. When he gets mad, he loses all self control."

"Cheyenne! Cheyenne! Jade shouted. Why don't you just go back! And please slow down!" "Why should I slow down," said Cheyenne. "Did I tell you to follow behind me?" Jade said to him, "I do know exactly how you feel. To tell you the truth, I want to find that gemstone myself, and for this nightmare to be over just as much as you do. Do you think that I don't want to go home? As long as Tribor, Komodo, and those corrupted armies of there's are still terrorizing the earth, we will never be able to go home! Cheyenne, please listen to me. Come back. And fight together with us. We all need you."

"Alright, Jade, you win this time. But remember this. If we don't find the gemstone, I am surely going my own separate way. This is taking too long. And my patience is wearing out! Why do the good have to suffer so badly? There are only five of us left, compared to only thousands of them. Do you think this is fair? Of course not! That's why we must succeed. We must win this battle.

This is what we were trained to be, warriors. And we should die as warriors. Not as cowards who turn their backs and walk away like me. Come on. Let's go back." Jade who was gleaming with happiness, took off into the air with her loyal companion Cheyenne, and they happily returned to the other fighters.

Chan told Cheyenne, "Welcome back!" They all gathered together to find out what the next step will be to help them locate the missing prism. Within seconds, a vision appeared to them. The glow became brighter and brighter. Hotei and the seven spirits of Buddha had come to help them. "My son. I have come to tell you all is not lost! You will obtain the stolen prism and get it back. It is in the hands of one of your arch enemies. That cunning vamp of Tribor's whom you have had an encounter with at the battlefield." "What! said Chan. You mean that sinister vamp who threatened to get back at me?" "Yes! Hotei said. But you must hurry before she gives it to Tribor. She has plans to become queen of the Realm Of Hell. Do not give in to her. Put lots of pressure and force for her to give you back the prism. Come, my son. I will go with you and the warriors to her hideout.

This will not be an easy task. For she is very powerful."

Hotei took Chan and the warriors to a dreadful place called the Valley Of Death.

The Valley Of Death was a deadly and deserted valley with lots of hills and mountains. There were lots of wild flowers which spreaded throughout the deserted valley.

There were also rows of wild hyacinth and wild geranium flowers everywhere also. The atmosphere of death was in the air. Ferocious black panthers, tigers, giant black widow spiders, and poisonous red scorpions roamed there. Even primitive barbarian apes dwelled on top of the hills ready to devour their prey.

"This is the place where all witches dwell. Be very careful my fighters, this place is very poisonous, said Hotei. I can tell this place is poisoned by the way it looks." "Yeah, it smells too," said Raseen. Hotei laughed.

"Are you expecting this place to be beautiful and clean? No way. We must protect all goodness in this world. This is what we are fighting for." "Hotei, do you know where this witch is at that fought with Chan?" said Jade. Hotei nodded his head to Jade. "Of course I do. I can locate any spirit in the entire universe. But this witch is clever and extremely dangerous. She knows its just a matter of time before someone will come after her. This is why we must have perfect timing and courage to defeat her. Are you fighters ready for the challenge? All the fighters said at the same time," "Yes!!" "Then lets get the prism of Nirvana!!" Hotei shouted. Hotei and the seven Buddhas began to fly into the sky. Each Buddha began to scan the area in seven different directions. "Do you think the Buddhas can find the witch?" Cheyenne said. "Remember, what Hotei said. We must have faith and patience. You all have to believe that! All of you!" Ming said. "You're right Ming. They are our only hope to win this fight against this type of of evil," Chan said. "I want to know Chan, what did you do to that witch anyway? Are you sure she doesn't like you for herself?" teased Chaka. "Of course not!" shouted Chan. "You never know about these types of things," she teased him again. "How can she have a crush on me! I turned her into ashes, Chaka. And boy! Is she mad!" "You know good and well you should not do these things to a woman," Chaka said.

"Wait a minute! I think I see the Buddha gods returning. Yes it is! They're coming back finally.

"We have searched extensively and discovered that the witch has her domain hidden on the high top of the hill at the Valley Of Death," said one of the seven Buddhas. "Alright! Let's teach this ugly tramp a lesson. Let's go!!" Cheyenne said excitedly. "No! It will soon be dark! We will stay here for tonight, and attack at dawn. Her powers will be much weaker," Hotei said. "What do you mean Hotei? Do you know there are panthers, tigers, black widow spiders, and red scorpions, ready to have us for lunch?" Raseen pointed out to Hotei. "Ha! Ha! Ha! Ha! Don't worry. There're harmless. You are a warrior. You are not afraid? Are you Raseen?" "Stop complaining Raseen, we're all together in this," said Jade. "Will you please shut up and go to sleep."

"I want to be able to kick butt, screamed Chaka. If you don't get enough rest, you will not be able to function. Everyone knows that. We have to be wide awake and alert for the big event tomorrow. And I will not lose, due to lack of sleep. Who knows? Maybe Buddha can do us a favor and whip us up a nice big breakfast."

Chapter Ten

Dawn came too soon. After a hearty breakfast, a surprise from Hotei and the other Buddha spirits, the warriors, along with their protective Buddha gods started out on the path to the Valley Of Death. It was a long and tiresome journey to the witches hill. Fighting off the fierce beasts, insects, and primitive men was not an easy task.

Thank the Buddha gods for being with them. After defeating their enemies, Chan gave praises to Buddha and the seven spirits. Sitting upon the highest hill was the nasty witch's domain. "Stay firm and keep alert!" Chan instructed to his men. As they approached the entrance to the cave, strange noises were heard. "Duck down!" Chan said screaming to his friends. Zap! Zap! Large fireballs were hurled at Chan and his men. The fiery fireballs were thrown left and right, one behind the other. "I can't see who is firing them!" Cheyenne said. "Look out! cried Chaka. Here comes another one!" "Whoever is throwing them, sure has good aim! Raseen said. And apparently they are invisible!" "Good thinking!" Jade said.

"Wait! said Chan. "I know what to do!" He put his hands up in front of him. The first fireball that came towards him, Chan with his hands held up, released a freezing beam which froze the fireballs.

It was suspended in mid air frozen solid. Each time the fireballs were swiftly released, Chan zapped them into a frozen fireball. Then, he reached into his pouch, and threw all around the cave some special dust. This dust was magical and could uncover anything invisible. There appeared ugly witches. All of them had white and silver hair. Their whole body, including their hideous faces, were green. Some had three crooked eyes instead of two. And their eyes were reddish green which would release fire from them. This is where the fiery fireballs came from. They got extremely mad when Chan froze their fireballs. So, they whipped out their long white and silver hair and extended it around Chan and his men's necks.

"We're being choked!" Ming gasped. "I can't breathe!" "This is a suffocation attack!" yelled Cheyenne. And it's even harder to tear the hair loose!" Directly out of the air, came a couple of little swords. These were cutting swords.

Each one were spiraling in the air and coming towards the warriors. The small and sharp spiraling swords began cutting the white and silver hair of the cold blooded witches, which released the warriors from their awful grip.

"Must be help from the Buddha! Jade said. They did say they would help us and be with us wherever we go. Thank you! Buddha. Thank you!" "Yes! We all thank Buddha!" they chimed in together. The leader of the witches Hepra saw what happened. She was mad with rage at how the Buddha gods helped Chan to escape death. "We shall see about this!" Hepra said.

"Nobody escapes here! I am the queen of the witches! And they shall see that there is no hope when you come in contact with me! "You have failed me!! Hepra madly screeched to her witch servants who threw the fireballs. "Now die for it!!" "NO!NO! screamed the servants. We have been loyal to you. Forgive us…" It was too late. Just that quick the cruel and cold blooded queen witch killed her servants. "That will be a warning to the rest of you who fails me!" she said. "Yes, my queen, we will obey your commands!! all her servants said. Please spare us my queen."

"Now go kill all of the warriors!! Use all powers I gave to you!!" Hepra demanded. The witch servants joined forces together and used their powers. They began to multiply right before the eyes of the fighters. And they grew in height. "Oh my word! Did you see that? I didn't know witches can do those sort of things! Unbelievable!" mumbled Raseen. "That's why they are witches Raseen. They have powers, Jade said to Raseen. "No talking! Go fight them!" Ming yelled at the fighters. The warriors used their martial arts techniques. They did their flying stances with all their kicking moves. But nothing effected the scary and grusome witch servants. They kept on multiplying. "I don't understand. Everything we used, is not taken enough effect.

Chan began to use his magical dust from his pouch. "Maybe this would work on them," Chan thought to himself. The evil servants kept on multiplying. "It's amazing! Everything we use on the witches servants just goes right through. It's just like we're not here," said Cheyenne.

Suddenly, out of nowhere, the seven Buddha's returned. The Buddha's flew in front of the warriors. "It's about time we get some help around here. We're running out of space!" exclaimed Raseen. One of the spirit Buddha's said, "These servants of the witch Hepra is using the dark magic stance.

You warriors cannot defeat this kind of black magic. We will use the light magic stance on them." The seven Buddha gods began to form a pyramid right in front of the warriors.

The buddha hands were placed in the praying position. "Look at that! HA!HA!HEEEE!! The gods are using the light magic stance, said one of the witchly servants. We are not stupid!"

Immediately, the Buddha's began to glow brighter and brighter. Soon the Buddha's were so bright, that the wicked servants started to expand and burst. “AAH!! Help me!” one of the witch servants shouted. “I can’t hold on any longer!” another one said. “The light is too bright!!”

It’s killing me and melting my eyes!!” All of the corrupted servants of Hepra were gone. They exploded with great and explosive force. Their pieces scattered in all directions.

“Excellent! Excellent! A job very well done, Buddha’s. So beautiful!” Hotei said with delight. He praised them over and over again. “I could not have done a better job than this myself!” Hotei said smiling. “EEEE-HEE HEE HEE!! How dare you Hotei, enter my dwelling and destroy all of my loyal subjects! You know you cannot interfere in our territory! Who give you the right to…” “Wait a minute queen Hepra! said Hotei. As you well know, Tribor started this. Is he playing true to the rules? No, he’s not. He created problems in Nirvana and now he’s making problems here on earth,” said Hotei. “Really? Hepra said. Do you think I care about this so called war? Tribor should take over the earth and claim what is his. I don’t blame him.”

Your so called heavenly being doesn’t care. If he did care, he wouldn’t send down these puny warriors. They can’t even fight my servants. And you Hotei, had to interfere. This is my fight with

Chan, not with you." "Well I am sorry you feel that way. If you want to fight with Chan, you will have to fight with me first. Then you can fight with Chan." That's the way it's going to be," Hotei said with a big smile on his face. Hepra was so outdone she began screaming her head off. "NO!!!!" She threw her hands in the air and a wild gush of wind began growing. Then the witch thrust all her magic at Hotei. "Now you, Hotei, will feel my raft," cackled the old witch. At that instant Hotei waved his right hand from left to right. The witch Hepra turned into a four year old child. Immediately afterwards, the whole entire dwelling place of the witches lair had transformed from an ugly and dark gloomy place to a beautiful and serene palace. "This is almost like Nirvana," one of the Buddha's said. He nodded with approval. "Yes isn't it," said Hotei.

I cannot believe all of this is happening. "How come we don't have this type of power?" Raseen said to Hotei. "You all do, Hotei replied back to Raseen. But, first you have to learn how to master it. Don't you have faith yet?" "But where is the prism?" Chan questioned. "Oh yes, the prism. I almost forgot," Hotei explained to Chan. "Hepra, give the prism back to Chan," Hotei told her. "Yes Hotei, I am sorry I took it," said Hepra as a little girl. Hepra walked up to Chan and gave the shiny prism back to him. “Remember warriors. This is only temporary. The palace will turn back evil again. You must defeat and destroy Tribor at all costs,” said one of the Buddha’s. “Yes time is running out,” another Buddha said. “But we don’t know where Tribor is,” said Chaka. “Don’t worry, said Hotei. Soon he will be found.”

Chapter Eleven

The Buddha gods sent Chan and his men back to the same place where the ancient broken down monastery was at. But waiting for them when they arrived was Ninjas. Black Ninjas. "Didn't we fight them from before? said Ming. I remember in the sutra book and in some of the picture scrolls, these Ninjas." "If they are defeated by their enemies, they will return and come back just as dangerous and trifling as before. Ninjas take a death vow. They also kill and kill in unarmed combat and armed combat. Even to their own shadows come alive. And their secret fighting art is revealed to no one. I do know two of the Ninja weapons which they use are called the chain and shuriken. "If these Ninjas are the same ones I read about, we are in real big trouble! This is called the revenge of the Ninjas," said Jade.

Little did they know, that some of them were invisible, and some had mind control powers. The first weapon had been thrown. Flaming sharp edged stainless steel throwing stars was thrown at the warriors. "Watch out!" yelled Chan. He caught each steel star in between each of his fingers. There was not a trace of blood coming from his fingers. He had gained more super magical powers since he was with the spirit

Buddha's. The Ninjas start spinning in circular motion with super fast speed towards the fighters. Chaka did a butterfly kick, and knocked out three of the spinning Ninjas. The ones that was invisible were flying, kicking, and biting everyone with their sharp teeth. It was so hard to fight the invisible ones back because they could not be seen! So Chan blew real hard from his breath a red dye in every direction of the invisible Ninjas, and they became visible like the rest. "Good! Now we can see!" said Ming.

"It's payback time!" Ming glides across in front of the Ninjas, stooping at the same time, while he glides and savagely slashes half of their legs off with his black and gold Dragon Scabbard Tai Chi sword.

The biggest fight was with the king of the Ninjas. He wanted to fight Chan very badly because he heard how good he was in his martial arts and a warrior man of great strength.

Said the revengeful Ninja to Chan, "Let's see how good you are man of Nirvana! I couldn't wait to challenge you to a good duel. And now the time has finally come. You think you are the grand master of martial arts. But you're not!"

I'm the grand master!" "You talk so big!" said Chan. Shut up and show me what you can do! I'm ready!!" Using two kitana swords at the same time, the Ninja leader charged at Chan, twisting, turning, spinning, and jumping in mid air. Chan pulled out his Lion Head Tai Chi sword. It was a lasered electrical sword, which shoots off high voltages of electricity. The force from the Tai Chi sword was so strong, it knocked the leader's sword right out of his hands. "Very good! said the Ninja leader. I'm impressed!"

Chan didn't pay him no mind. He quickly opened up the Bamboo Black Fan and waved it vigorously. This made the Ninja leader dizzy. He was in a daze. While the fan was in motion, Chan held up his wrist and released several pointy and sharp steel spikes. These were Chan's throwing spikes which were attached to a wrist strap. The killer spikes penetrated into the head, heart, and chest of the Ninja leader, killing him instantly.

After the tireless fight with the Ninjas, the warriors decide to take a break. Raseen decides to sit upon a blue rock for support. As soon as he sat upon the blue rock, Raseen fell into some time warp. "AAHH! AAHH! Help!" screamed Raseen. He was falling into a deep cave. This cave was no ordinary cave. There was giant one-eyed ogres of the underworld. They were also dreadful monsters who feeds on human beings. Carried on their shoulders were huge battle axes used to stomp their enemies to death. When Raseen landed in the caves of the ogres, all of them ran towards him at rapid speed to stamp him until his death.

For this was fresh meat. Raseen, fearing for his life, began leaping and flying through the air throwing punches, kicks, and blocking techniques. "Boy! These suckers are so big!" Raseen said to himself. Using the tumbling technique, he rolled over and over with great speed like a bowling ball until he made the one-eyed ogres fall to the ground. Some of them fell to the ground with a loud thump! The ogres growled furiously at Raseen. They swished their battle axes as hard as ever at his body. But Raseen wanted to survive.

This is no time for fear to overcome him. He is suppose to act and fight like a true warrior. Raseen threw with all his might poisonous missile darts at every part of their bodies. The darts were red and yellow with a poisoned pointed shaft at one end, and green, blue, and purple feathers attached at the other end. The angry ogres uttered a high shrill piercing cry. The highly toxic poison from the darts was settling in their system. It was a matter of seconds, and all of them fell dead.

Meanwhile, Chan and his men searched frantically for Raseen.

He was no where to be found. Chan used his scanning device.

The device picked up sounds from the blue rock Raseen had been sitting on. He turned the dial on the gadget to full strength. There was a vision of Raseen in the cave of the ogres. Chan used his special telepathy voice to communicate to Raseen. "Raseen! Raseen! Don't worry! I am going to get you out. Be patient!" "I hear you loud and clear! said Raseen shouting in the air to Chan. But do try to hurry."

Without hesitation, Chan magnetized the blue rock with his neutrons from his device. A large hole was made in the earth. Then Chan beamed Raseen back up to them, just like a magnet. "Boy! Am I ever glad to see you! Raseen said. I felt like a hot potato! And I almost was dinner. Or was it lunch?" The others patted him on the back. They all were glad to see him. Chan laughed. "Did you come to any danger while you were down there?" "I sure did! There were giant man eating ogres with huge battle axes, ready to crush me!" said Raseen. And I destroyed them by using my highly poisonous darts." "Good, good said Chan. You are becoming a brave and studious warrior. I am proud of you. And you defended yourself well. I couldn't of done a better job myself. Do you realize now the skills will come to you once you have total and complete faith in yourselves. The Buddha will always be with you during hard times and good times. Just hold your head up high and be proud to be a warrior. This is one title you keep for the rest of your life. So, be proud of what you are, and especially who you are. It is your fears sometimes that hold you back from doing the right thing. Once you conquer your fears, the doors will open."

The warriors were trying to figure out the correct path to take which would lead them to Tribor and the Realm Of Death And Hell. As they proceeded to walk straight ahead, it began to snow, and hail. The winds were very strong, and kept blowing them back each time they tried to move ahead.

The snow got deeper and deeper. "What is this? Cheyenne shouted out loud. Why all of sudden we walked into bad weather? This must be some kind of mirage! There's an evil force out there that wants us to turn back, or give up." "I noticed that too, Jade said. It's too much of a coincidence that when we started walking, a big storm came along. Something is not right! This happens to us every time we get ready to try to find the path which can lead us to the realm of hell." Ming, Chan, Raseen, Chaka, and Cheyenne seemed baffled by this also. At that quick moment, the storm stopped. But the ground was still covered from the heavy falling of the snow.

"Where are we at? It looks like we are in some type of mountainous region. But how did we manage to wind up in this place?" said Chaka. "I bet when we were being blinded by the snow storm and all that hail, we walked far out of the way into this dismal place," Ming said to his companions. "Well, let's walk more further and see where it leads to." As soon as Ming tried to lift up his feet to walk, he couldn't. His legs got very stiff.

Chapter Twelve

So stiff, he couldn't move them. The others had the same problem. And even to their bodies began to feel cold and rigid. Chaka was not easily heeled over by this. She kept struggling and trying to push her feet forward as best as she could. Even to her legs began stifling. The other warriors started to freeze more too. If something wasn't done fast, they would all become frozen ice people. Jade began to cry because all this coldness was aching her bones with such severity. Ming thought about his magical lasso.

"I got an idea! he called out to the fighters. Don't worry!

Soon we will be released from this frozen ice. Just bare with me here for a few seconds. One of my arms did not get stiff yet." "That's so good to hear! All the fighters called out to Ming. We know you will try to get us out of this mess!" "Oh my lord! screamed Jade. Look at Chaka! She has frozen solid like an ice statue. And also Jade. You could see the frozen teardrop upon her icy face. What sort of madness is this? Hurry Ming! Hurry!" Ming whipped out with all the energy he had left, his ultraviolet lasso out of his pocket belt. There was a secret compartment which held it tightly and in place. The purple ultraviolet lasso whipped on top of the frozen feet of Ming. It penetrated deep into the ice. Then the ice melted rapidly, releasing Ming's entire body from its frozen state. Then he whipped and swayed the long lasso towards Chan so the burning rays from the lasso would remove the freeze from him. He did this to each warrior. Cheyenne, Jade, and Chaka. This weapon cut at the ice like glass. Breaking it into thousands of tiny broken fragments. The spell of the ice storm was over.

"Whew!! Raseen said. I never want to experience that again!

You actually felt like an iceberg. And Jade, you really looked good as a block of ice. Jade, Jade." Raseen kept on calling her. As he turned around, he realized she had fainted to the ground. She had frostbite. There was still some ice left on her. Apparently, she did not completely defrost. "Help her! Somebody do something before she becomes frostbitten and dies! We can't afford to lose another fighter, squealed Chaka. We need her!" "Don't panic! Chan said. He went into his mystic pouch and unfolded what seemed to be a cloak. It was a thermal cloak.

It was designed exclusively for situations like this one. When placed on the frozen victim, it would bring back their proper body heat temperature. Chan hastily placed the cloak on

Jade's weak body. The thermal cloak got warmer and warmer. There was a groaning and moaning noise coming out of her mouth. She started talking out of her head. "Come on! Come on! You can do it! shouted Cheyenne. Be strong!"

Jade was really a strong person. Soon she came out of it.

"Where am I? What happened? Is this some kind of joke? What am I'm doing all covered up like this. Cheyenne explained to her everything that had happened. It was hard to try and convince Jade that this was not her fault she could not come out of the ice so easily like the others. Things sometimes he reasoned with her happens this way. "What about the rest of you? Are you all alright?" "Sure. Sure we are Jade, said Ming. The best thing is that are better now. That's what counts. That is why we all must stick together. Sister and brother team. Brotherly love. Right Chan? "Right! said Chan. The sooner we all stick to that motto, the more we can appreciate each other and respect each others feelings.

Love conquers all. Except for a few exceptions. Tribor.

When it comes to love, that's something he does not have and does not know how to give. I really do think it's too late for him. He's got too much of the dark side in him now. You could turn him inside out, and he will always stay the way he is. Scrupulous, cunning, wicked, provocative, arrogant, and most of all heartless. I even think that is gone. He was kicked down into hell by our angels from the holy city of Nirvana, and he will continue to be in hell.

Some people you cannot change. And then again, they may not want to change. The evilness gets good to them."

Once the magical ultraviolet lasso touched the ice the whole entire region became unfrozen. They were able to walk the grounds again, and used their legs without any difficulty.

It also started to warm up. This is a great break for the warriors.

The warriors continued their walk along the grassy trails.

It was so much better now that they had started again to try to find the road which would lead them to Tribor. This was their regular routine. Try to find the right trail or path that would take them to the realm of hell. Far, far, far into the horizon they slowly walked. And it got hot. It got hotter and hotter. The brilliance of the sun's rays made it feel just like it was a high temperature of 104 degrees. The fighters sweat glands were working rapidly. The warriors pressed ahead. Each step they took, felt like hot coals on their feet, face, and their body. “Does anybody knows where the cool spot is? I can’t believe its so hot!” Raseen said slowly. “I thought you were from India Raseen?”

You should be use to this kind of heat. It’s usually hot in India,” replied Chaka. “I know what kind of weather they have in India. You don’t have to remind me of that! I’ll tell you this, it’s much more cooler in India than here!” yelled Raseen. “Why, it’s not hot! Just think of winter.

Imagine an igloo,” said Ming. “In this type of heat, that ice would melt in one second. “Does anybody have any water?” said Jade. “Jade, is there something wrong with you? Where are we going to find water out here? Humph! Tribor could be any place and she is looking for water. Some women!” replied Raseen. “You know some water would taste pretty good right about now,” Cheyenne said. “All of you listen to me. We can’t stop any longer. We have to hurry up and stop Tribor now. Just look at the prism. Chan opened his hands to show the prism. It began to blink wildly with different colors. “I never saw the gemstone turned like that! What does it mean Chan?” questioned Cheyenne. “Your guess is as good as mine. I don’t know. I bet you we are very close to that evil thing,” answered Chan. “You are right Chan, lets keep going. Humanity is counting on us,” Chaka said. Ming said cheerfully to his men, “You know guys, I agree with Jade on this one. We really need water right about now.

Have you seen the trails? It’s really beginning to crack due to lack of water. This place even looks like my village back at home.” “Amen for that! Cheyenne blurted out. Now let’s keep moving. There’s no time for gossip.”

Again, the fighters moved on. As they walked across the dry deserted land, they saw different kinds of dead carcasses.

Some were dead birds, animals, and human remains. Along with that came the foul odors. “What is this? The Valley Of The Dead? said Raseen. “You know, this is too much! Everywhere you look, you see these dead things hanging around. I’m ready to go home. What I would do to be in my own bed right now. With the bed covers pulled over my head.” Cheyenne bought out a great idea to the warriors.

This could be the main territory of Tribor. Just think about it. All these dead carcasses and bodies or what have you. This would be the kind of place a man of that sinister type of character would choose.” “Wait! Jade spoke out. I think I see something straight ahead. Maybe it’s a clue to this place.” “Let’s go!!” Ming said, as he flew across the deserted land.” “Wait a minute Ming! It might be a mirage! yelled Chan to Ming. The heat plays tricks on your mind sometimes." "Chan, I swear. I thought I saw something out there. It might be a clue. Trust me." Ming said with joy in his voice. As soon as they got there, the clue he seen disappeared. "That's strange. I don't see a thing now.

And I know I did see something move right about here at this spot. You were right Chan, this was certainly a mirage! Me and my stupid self. I should of known better. It must be the heat."

Immediately, Ming and Chan flew back where the others were at. "Well Ming, where is your famous clue? I know you wouldn't find anything out there. Why would Tribor give us any clues anyway? You know how much he hates us! Some fighter you are," Raseen said with a smirk. "Okay, okay you win. Know what? I think we really need to stop. I can't go on. I'm so hot and tired," Chaka said with a weak voice.

"You can make it Chaka. We're just about to enter his main territory. Have more Chi," Chan said. "Chan, to be really honest, I really don't think I can hold on much longer."

At that moment Chaka collapses in Cheyenne's arms. "She's really hot. She doesn't look too good Chan. I think she needs medical attention," Cheyenne said to Chan. "Oh no!! gasped Chan. Look at the sky! It's turning purple, or something.

And look at that! Something is coming out!" "Maybe it's Tribor's pets, looking for food and we are it!" yelled Raseen. "Quick! Run behind the cactuses, so whatever it is doesn't see us!" yelled Ming excitedly.

Chapter Thirteen

Purple clouds which was very, very big emerged in the sky. Excessive lightning and thundering surrounded the clouds. The color of the clouds got darker and darker. The color changed into a darker deeper purple which made the clouds look black. Heavy fog mist was circling around it. Chaka gasped in fright. "I have never seen such a sight of pure wickedness. Not even in my own village have I seen an apparition so awesome." The dark purple clouds began to descend to the grounds below. The ground shook violently as if it was ready to explode. The earth split open. When the earth widely opened, an enormous gust of black smoke arose from it, and steaming lava mist. Raseen whispered, "So this is how you get to Tribor's hideout! No wonder we couldn't find it! It was hidden out of nowhere!" "SHH! SHH! Be quiet!" said Jade. Someone might hear you! We cannot be discovered by Tribor or his men until Chaka is revived." "She's absolutely right! agreed Chan. We can't mess up now.

We are taking a big risk hiding behind these cactuses. And it's still hot!! That's why Tribor probably put his secret passage here in a deserted hot place. No one can tolerate this heat! One thing

I do give him credit for. He is a clever and intelligent guy. You have to be to think of a location such as this one." There was only one thing on Chan's mind. To revive poor helpless Chaka. And this was a good time to for all of them to climb down into the huge crater hole before it closes. Chan used smelling salts, and some of his special herbal medicine to bring her back to life. A few prayers were said over her body as she laid there looking asleep. There was a little cough, and then a loud cough. Each cough got stronger. Chaka was coming around to her senses. Chan gave her another dosage of his herbal medicine. When she awoke she was glad to see her friends. "Where are we? Chaka said. I don't remember anything." "You fainted back there," Cheyenne told her.

It was too hot a climate for you. And it grows even hotter. There's a big crater hole in the earth and we have to climb in it, before it completely shuts closed. We all think this is lord Tribor's secret passage to his hideout and the realm of hell. If we are right, we have made the biggest and most important discovery of our lives! Now that you have survived this terrible fainting spell, we can proceed and go on ahead and climb down into the hole. This is the only way to get in. But Tribor and his men must not see us. We have to stay out of sight. I'm really surprised they didn't check behind these cactuses. Since he's suppose to be so smart. By the way, are you feeling strong enough to walk now?" "I feel just fine! said Chaka. She stands up. "But my legs feel a little bit weak. Thanks!"

The warriors carefully sneaked into the large crater hole holding their noses because of the great vapor steam. "Its like taking a steam bath! laughed Raseen. Without the bubbles!" Everyone laughed. Sweat began dripping off the faces of the warriors. It was so hot you could hardly breathe. This was terrible. The warriors felt as if they were suffocating. Deeper and deeper into the hole they went. There were skeleton bones all around the place and whispering voices of the dead. Their spirit was swarming around. A cold chill ran up and down Chan's spine. He had a bad feeling about all this. This was a creepy dwelling.

There was creepy small insects and reptiles crawling busily everywhere. Different sections and pathways divided the halls. It was very easy to get lost. All these curves, made you crazy. Haunting sounds put fear in you. Some parts were very dark. You couldn't even see your hands. A green and black small iguana crawled upon Jade's back. She tried not to panic. Whatever it was, she could barely see it. But she managed to fling it off from her back without going into a fit. As they turned around a certain corridor, it got a little brighter. There were hanging torches on every part of the wall. And the odor became unbearable. Chan and his warriors decided to explore the place more further.

A lot of twists and turns of almost every corner in the dark hole led them to a dead end. It seemed like it took forever.

Just then, one of the fighters spotted a light at the end of the tunnel. The smell of fresh air hit their noses. They followed the light, and continued on until they reached the end where the light was. "See! See! I knew this would lead us to the way out!" shouted Ming. All the warriors climbed their way out into the broad daylight. Raseen was the last one to climb out. "Hey! We got company! said Chan. Look around us!" This was true. As soon as they climbed out of the hole, there was Tribor, Komodo and their armies of men surrounding them. Just that quick a red sonic laser beam came out from Tribor's eyes, striking at every warrior, in all directions. But they managed to escape the fiery and awsome rays by jumping and leaping out of the way. Komodo sent out his giant claw hands, which wildly stretched and clutched the warriors with great force. Sometimes he would furiously whip out his vicious tongue. Or nastily spit his poisonous and acidity toxic saliva at them. Still, very previously hurt from his last combat, Chan put up a good fight. But he still needed his wounds to be taken care of immediately. So, he pulled out his precious gemstone prism of Nirvana. It has amazing healing powers. It works better than the herbal medicine. Just by touching it, all his bad wounds healed rapidly right before their eyes. Nothng now at this point can hurt him or grasp him. Chan stretches out his hands so the prism stone would reflect on his companions and heal them also. "No! Raseen cries out. Forget about us and get Tribor. We will stay and try to defeat Komodo." Jade said, "Finish the mission! The fullest blue moon is about to become full! Look!" Tribor, looking up into the sky frantically realized the warrior was right. The fullest blue moon was just about to change into it's new phase.

Realizing this he vanishes. Chan calls out to Tribor. "Where are you hiding, Tribor? Are you scared?" As swiftly as he could, Chan holds up the prism of Nirvana. Like a crystal ball, the prism's vibrant rays showed him where the evil Tribor had escaped to. A strange purplish glow had surrounded Chan's entire body and he by himself, instantly was transported to the final realm. Tribor's Realm Of Death And Hell. There was Tribor waiting for his arch enemy. He knew he would come after him. Neither one wasted their time. The two enemies fought violently with their martial arts weapons and magical sorcery. Both of them had superb extraordinary skills and were a perfect match for each other. Tribor had excellent training from the holy land heavenly city of Nirvana before he turned wicked. And Chan had superior training from the Buddha gods of Shaolin. This was not going to be easy. The Violet Flame Sword was what Chan decided to use to defeat Tribor once and for all. He thrusted with all his might, his flaming sword into the master of evil heart, and skillfully used the fire of destruction technique to kill him for eternity. Tribor yelled out in agony for he was in extreme pain. This was a pain he had never felt before. Holding up the prism of Nirvana, Chan recited the sorcery spell for eternal and final destruction. "I command you Tribor, in the name of Nirvana, and the prism of Nirvana, for your wickedness and body to be no more. So, mote it be!" The prism shook with great force. All the neutron power of every color from the rays of the prism, zapped Tribor's body. Tribor melts and mysteriously vaporizes. Chan, assuming the job was done, walks away very tired. He starts to stumble from weakness and exhaustion.

The kingdom of Tribor's Realm Of Death And Hell was coming to an end. The deadly realm from the massive earthquake falls apart. Walls began to cave in. The grounds shook tremendously. Every single man of Komodo's and Tribor's organization had burned and disintegrated. Even back at the site where the other warriors were fighting with Komodo and his army of darkness, they all vanished. Power was lost because of the death of their leader. "Jade! Jade!" yelled Chaka. "Where could she be?" said Cheyenne. "I'm afraid I have some bad news for you, Raseen said. I looked back as we were running and saw one of the zombie men attack Jade, and before I could do anything, poof! she vanishes into thin air! Don't worry. We will find a way to get her back. Let's wait for Chan. He will know what to do. That is, if he's still alive."

Back in Tribor's world, in the Realm Of Death And Hell, everything was falling under. Chan runs to save himself from being buried alive. The dark and fiery Realm Of Death And Hell was exploding profusively. Loud explosions and hot, hot lava bought the hell hole to its doom. Screams were rampant everywhere. It seems there were no escape or hope for the tomb of darkness.

Chan thought his mission of destroying Tribor and his kingdom was over. The world and the heavenly Nirvana he thought is now safe. But it was not over. Not by a long shot. There is a time in life when we make mistakes. Small ones and big ones. But that's the purpose of making these mistakes. So we can learn from them. And, then again because of our being over anxious, we leave things undone or unnoticed. One thing Chan did not notice when he walked away was Tribor's spirit had left out of his body, and went inside of one of the blood sucking flesh eating vampires.

When Chan recited the spell of eternal destruction, he forgot to mention for the spirit of Tribor to be no more.

All that was mentioned when he recited the spell was the evilness and body to be no more. This mistake was not done intentionally, but it was very costly. The blood thirsty vampire slowly lifts up his head. His beady and sinister eyes glows with a red fiery glow. Tribor laughs a hideous and piercing loud laugh. But Chan did not hear it. He was too exhausted and worn out from this mission. To him, all was well. And his mission had finally been accomplished.

With his final breath, Tribor cackles with his sinister voice, "I will be back and get my revenge!! Wait and see!

"Holy man of Nirvana!"

THE END

About the Author

Venessa Williamson is an aspiring actress, singer, and writer of children's books and screenplays. She is a native of New York City. Her hobbies are writing and collecting dolls from foreign countries. Being a single parent as well, she enjoys her spare time with her two children going to concerts, dancing, and playing software games, and reading the bible.

Deserie Questell is also an aspiring actress, singer, and writer of screenplays, and the sister of Venessa Williamson. She is a native of New York City. Deserie is currently a student at the U.S.A. Shaolin Temple in Manhattan, N.Y. where she is practicing Kung Fu and Tae Kwon Do. She in her spare time has done TV and film roles.

www.ingramcontent.com/pod-product-compliance
Ingram Content Group UK Ltd.
Pitfield, Milton Keynes, MK11 3LW, UK
UKHW041821200726
13854UKWH00001BA/261